# A VOICE OVER THE WATER

# A
# VOICE
# OVER
# THE
# WATER

## An Invitation
## to Pray

# WILLIAM
# BREAULT, s.j.

Ave Maria Press
Notre Dame, Indiana 46556

Unless otherwise indicated, all scriptural passages are from the *Good News Bible*, © American Bible Society, 1976.

> Notation for other versions:
> JB *Jerusalem Bible*
> NIV *New International Version*
> RSV *Revised Standard Version*

© 1985 by Ave Maria Press

All rights reserved. No part of this publication may be reproduced, stored in a retrieval system, or transmitted, in any form or by any means, electronic, mechanical, photocopying, recording, or otherwise, without the written permission of the publisher, Ave Maria Press, Notre Dame, Indiana 46556.

Library of Congress Catalog Card Number: 84-73051

International Standard Book Number: 0-87793-280-8 (Cloth)
0-87793-281-6 (Paper)

Cover design: Elizabeth French

Printed and bound in the United States of America

Photography:

Jan Gumprecht Bannan, 55, 69; Ron Byers, 23; Ron Carlson, 30; Patricia Coyner, 74; Bob and Miriam Francis, 14; Philip Gendreau, 110; Carole Graham, 102; Jean-Claude Lejeune, 66; David Mansell, 92; Bruce Roberts, cover, 51; Joan Sauro, 46; Lee Snider, 98; Vernon Sigl, 19, 25, 38, 43, 61, 81, 104; Justin Soleta, 78.

## ACKNOWLEDGMENTS

The thoughts expressed in this book were originally prepared for television. With the encouragement of Charles Jones and Frank Cunningham, both of Ave Maria Press, the ideas were put into book form as an aid to prayer.

I'd like to thank Paula Vigil for giving me considerable help with the manuscript and for a number of ideas which I have included in it.

# CONTENTS

The sea is mentioned many times in scripture as a place where God's word is felt in a special, creative way. The very first pages of the Hebrew scriptures speak of his word as hovering over the dark waters; and the parting of the sea was seen as a mighty act of God, a saving event in the history of a people. As such, it was wondered about and prayed over, not simply remembered. It became a further means of union with God. Jonah, that humorous prophet sent to the city of Nineveh, heard God's word and finally responded to it *in* the water, in the stomach of the whale. He prayed about it too. It changed his direction and his life since it was calling him to conversion.

The disciples of Jesus Christ were called from the shore of the sea of Galilee. From their boats he proclaimed the word, the good news of life. When the Lord's disciple, Peter, first heard the word to let his net down into the sea for a catch of fish he knew was not there, he may have doubted, yet he obeyed. From the miraculous catch of fish which followed, he saw deeply into the Lord's heart—and into his own.

The Lord walked to his disciples over the sea. Peter, acting on Christ's word, also walked on the water. And even though he began to sink, still he grew in trust by his prayer, "Lord, save me!"

Throughout scripture the word is often associated with water and God's Spirit. "No one can enter the Kingdom of God unless he is born of water and the Spirit." The Lord himself was in the water when a voice from heaven proclaimed, "You are my own dear Son. I am pleased with you." Again the sea was one of the chosen meeting places after the resurrection. Perhaps one of the reasons for the association between the word and water is the fact that the sea is somehow the source of life just as the word is. Both are a privileged place where something can flourish and come forth. A poet would say of the sea that its peaceful rhythms lure us away from our own worries and anxieties. In the sea—and in the word—we are confronted with a mystery that has preceded us and will carry on after us. Often, as a result, our own restlessness is gathered together and dissipated. The sea speaks a word and we listen.

A Voice Over The Water is a book of reflections which, it is hoped, will also speak a word. As the sea invites us to be still and listen, so I hope will this book of prayer.

There is no set time for praying, except when you are invited. And the initiative is always God's: When you are invited, pray. In using this book you needn't read through an entire section or page if something moves you to reflection or prayer before you get to the end. When that happens—and you should grow sensitive in recognizing it—try closing the book for a few moments, allowing yourself to feel and become aware of what has moved you. Give yourself permission to respond to God in your own words or by your silence. There is no need to read further. You can do that later. The book will always be there; the invitation to prayer might not be. Hurried reading often results in insensitivity, a strange sense of dryness from merely consuming words. I have often found myself moved to prayer while reading. Instead of listening to the invitation, I frequently kept on reading, reasoning that where there is something good something better will surely follow—and the moment of invitation passed me by! The better thing would have been to put the book aside for a few moments and digest the food I was being offered.

There is an unorthodox table of contents in the book. Look it over. If you see something that interests you, open the book to that section and get quiet in God's presence. Read, then pray. Pay special attention to the scripture quotation at the beginning of each chapter. Read it thoughtfully before looking at the reflection which follows. After having read or prayed over the thoughts suggested—or your own—you might try slowly rereading the scripture quote. Hopefully it will open up some of its meaning for you.

You needn't start at the beginning of the book and read straight through to the end. It might even be a hindrance to prayer to do so. Start where you want.

# ONE

# Mary's Prayer of Wonder

*The angel came to her and said, "Peace be with you! The Lord is with you and has greatly blessed you!"*

Luke 1:28

This is not a bad way to start a morning. Think of it: a message from an angel. A greeting of peace. The assurance that God is with you and even likes you! And a blessing.

Yet look at Mary's response:

Mary was deeply troubled . . . and she wondered (Lk 1:29).

Wonder is the heart of prayer, pondering the meaning of things: of messengers from God, of his presence hidden within, of countless blessings, of pain and love. This kind of prayer is not a one-time thing with Mary.

When the shepherds came across the early-morning fields to see the newly-born child, and when they themselves were filled with wonder, telling everyone they met about him, the scripture says of Mary that she "remembered all these things and thought deeply about them" (Lk 2:19).

Mary's basic stance toward life was that of a person of prayer: She wondered, thought deeply, reflected, remembered, pondered.

When she brought the child to the temple, the old man Simeon spoke a prophecy about him saying he would be a sign of contradiction, revealing our secret thoughts. Once more Mary wondered. Who wouldn't if such a thing were said about her newborn child?

She wondered about herself, too, for Simeon had turned to her and looking deeply into her still unclouded eyes said, "and sorrow, like a sharp sword, will break your own heart."

Prayer is to have your heart broken into, revealing your innermost thoughts.

But not in the way you expect.

*"Your father and I have been terribly worried trying to find you."*

Luke 2:48

When Jesus decided at 12 years old to stay in Jerusalem while the rest of the family continued home, he quite naturally upset his parents. When they found him later, his mother said, "Son, why did you do this to us? Your father and I have been terribly worried trying to find you."

Jesus' answer did nothing to alleviate his mother's concern. In fact it probably heightened it. "Didn't you know that I had to be in my Father's house?"

Of course she did! That is why she came back to Jerusalem to find him and bring him back home.

Another event to be pondered.

Another thing to be wondered about, trying to tease out of it God's meaning for her and her family.

*So Jesus went back with them to Nazareth, where he was obedient to them.*

Luke 2:51

Another event to be pondered: This child who clearly demonstrated that he had his own power and authority rooted in his relationship to his Father, returned with Mary and Joseph "where he was obedient to them" and was subject to their authority once again. Scripture says she treasured all these things in her heart, but the outcome of all this pondering, prayer and reflection was neither doubt, nor indecision. Wonder doesn't lead that way, nor does prayer. The one who prays does not become defiant or depressed because reality doesn't explain itself in what seems to be a contradiction in one's life. True prayer ends with trust and confidence—even joy—even when it's painful. Have you ever noticed that some of the psalms seem depressing (Psalm 88 or 90) yet they always end on an upbeat note of trust, even joy? It is the joy of the cross: There is something in the cross besides the obvious contradiction. Prayer homes in on that "something." So Mary could sing, like the psalmist:

> My heart praises the Lord;
>> my soul is glad because of God my
>> Savior.
>> For he has remembered me, his lowly
>> servant!
> From now on all people will call me
>> happy,
>> because of the great things the Mighty
>> God has done for me.
> His name is holy.

Luke 1:46-49

13

This child was a thorn in her heart, an open wound—as he is in ours often enough. But through that open wound life is poured out for others. It is kept open by prayer.

# TWO

# Getting Out of the Fast Lane

*His mother treasured all these things in her heart.*

Luke 2:51

Prayer starts from the heart. It takes place there. That is where the treasure is. That is also where the kingdom is and the king.

The heart is a room. And the door to that room must be periodically closed just to get the kind of privacy needed to be quiet. The door that must be closed is the one that seems to be constantly open to urgency—do this, now! Next, do that! Now, this!—a never-ending series of demands. Too many distractions (the word means to pull apart) make us insensitive to people and beauty around us. We grow calloused. There is no room for intimacy in a heart that is distracted and pulled apart constantly by the freeway pace of life.

Life in the fast lane! Often it's not life at all, just speed: foot pressed to the gas pedal, eyes intent on the car in front, to the side, the back. Shuttered, tunnel vision.

It is easy to miss the countryside traveling in the fast lane. When that happens, the heart dries up. There are no treasures left in it, so there is nothing left to treasure.

Prayer is being intimate with God, and that means slowing down. So there is a place for closing the door to the heart, for going off by oneself. To be alone. Re-created. To be silent.


*He went up a hill by himself to pray.*

Matthew 14:23


Silence is indispensable for prayer.

Silence is a reality in itself, not the absence of a reality: After all the noise stops, *then* there is silence. Real silence is not something that happens *after*.

It happens *before*. Before Mary conceives, there is a silence. Before the artist creates, a silence, a period of gestation.

Silence is that out of which comes something: presence and life. We ourselves flow forth from the creative silence of God.


*There came the sound of a gentle breeze.*

1 Kings 19:12 (JB)


The prophet Elijah ran for his life to get away from Queen Jezebel who had threatened to kill him. He went into the wilderness and prayed to die. That's how depressed he was! Finally he reached a cave and hid there, fearful and waiting. What he was waiting for soon came along: the word of God. He was told to go outside of the cave and wait for the appearance of God. When he did a mighty wind tore up the mountains, but God

16

wasn't in that wind. Next came an earthquake that ripped apart the land. After that, a fire destroyed what was left over. God was in none of them, so once again Elijah (who knew what violence was) stood outside of the cave waiting and along came the sound of a gentle breeze. God was in that!

One must be silent to hear the sound of a gentle breeze.

Silent, like the images Isaiah uses to describe the fruitful activity of God's word in our hearts:

> Yes, as the rain and the snow come down
>    from the heavens
> and do not return without watering the
>    earth,
> making it yield,
> and giving growth to provide seed for the
>    sower
> and bread for the eating,
> so the word that goes from my mouth
> does not return to me empty,
> without carrying out my will
> and succeeding in what it was sent to do.
> Isaiah 55:10-11 (JB)

As the Lord Jesus said during his 40 days of silence in the desert: "Man cannot live on bread alone, but needs every word that God speaks" (Mt 4:4).

The word of God in silence is a source of life.

THREE

# Convincing God

*"In your prayers do not use a lot of meaningless words. . . . Your Father already knows what you need before you ask him."*

Matthew 6:7-8

All those words. Are they formulas? Rituals for getting control of God? For influencing him? By way of an answer, Christ says simply, "Your Father already knows what you need before you ask him."

It is surprising how we persist in the idea that our prayer can control God! We inform him about what is going on and call his attention to what he should, after all, be concerned about. Maybe we even remind him of his duty:

"God, don't you see what is happening? Things are going from bad to worse. And now my wife is sick."

A prayer like this assumes that God is ignorant and has to be informed. Our prayer informs him, does something to him, makes him smarter, or tries to convince him to change his mind. And we're not above a bribe slipped into our prayer either.

"Please, God! This is important. You've got to listen to me. I might lose my job. You can change that, Lord. You're all-powerful! You've got to—I'll even give up_____."

There are many variations of the above prayer. Each person has his or her own. But prayer is not to change God. It is to be changed by God—maybe that's why some of us avoid it. Way back in the instinctive zones of our brains is the conviction that if we keep on praying something will happen to us.

And that is correct, for all prayer has one thing in common: a conversion. That is the occupational hazard of praying. But it isn't God who is converted, we are. Perhaps that is why we hold to the illusion that prayer does something to God. We don't want to be converted!

But God doesn't let up easily.

*"Ask and you will receive; seek, and you will find; knock, and the door will be opened to you. For everyone who asks will receive, and anyone who seeks will find, and the door will be opened to him who knocks."*

Matthew 7:7-8

The door the Lord is talking about starts out closed. And it is opened by knocking and seeking. That is what prayer is: a two-way process. Talking, seeking, asking; then, listening and waiting. The door opens.

Mary pondered the events in her life. But that is not the same as an instant and fixed recording of the event, like the flash of a photographer's camera; then a storage of the event in the memory bank. Pondering has to do with turning events over in the mind and heart. There is wonder in it, fear, doubt, hope—above all, the search for the hidden one.

What events? Those that make up your daily life.

*Pray at all times.*

1 Thessalonians 5:16

When people say they have tried prayer and given it up, it usually means that the outside world hasn't changed as a result of their prayer and they have stopped listening to the inside world. "My boy is still sick. My superintendent still dislikes me. You're not listening!"

And what do you do when people don't listen? Unplug them!

Listening is hard work. The illusion that we are—and must be—in control of everything that happens in our lives often keeps us from seeing this fact. We want results, and if our words and subtle bribes don't produce them, why pray?

20

But prayer is deeper than words. It's a relationship.

Does it work? Can you see results? You must look within for the answer, but only after having prayed for a while. If after praying you begin to sense more "focus" in your life, more peace, and a greater ability to cope, if you begin to see yourself and others through the compassionate eyes of Christ, if you start dealing with problem areas you would rather avoid, then *something* is going on. And it's going on within you. A door has opened. Something has been received. Something found. Better, Someone.

*He came to his own country, but his own people did not receive him.*

John 1:11

A cup must be empty before it can be filled. If it is already full, it can't be filled again except by emptying it out. In order to fill anything, there must be a hollowed-out space. Otherwise it can't receive.

This is especially true of God's word. In order to receive it, we must be hollowed out. We must be capable of receiving it, emptied of the false self and its endless demands.

When Christ came, there was no room in the inn. It was full.

The inn is a symbol of the heart. God's word, Christ, can take root only in a hollow.

# FOUR

# Coming Home

*At that time Jesus was filled with joy by the Holy Spirit and said, "Father, Lord of heaven and earth! I thank you because you have shown to the unlearned what you have hidden from the wise and learned."*

Luke 10:21

People move faster today than they did yesterday.

The reason why is easy to discover: increased means of communication. Radio, television, telephone, cars, airplanes—and right around the corner, computer space travel. All these things have increased the pace of our lives.

The ability to move faster and communicate more quickly often seems to turn into the compulsion to do so. There are meetings to attend, committees, clubs, social gatherings, places to go, things that *must* be done.

All too soon life begins to resemble a growing network of steel strands, always growing and never finished. What started as a convenience—even a pleasure—becomes a burden. And we become so weighed down that we no longer see. Sometimes we can no longer even believe in anything beyond the immediate goal that compels us to act! That is when the heart dries up. Emptied. Burned out and insensitive.

When this happens, we must stop, get quiet, and look beyond our own small world to the larger world we are so much a part of. And this requires a moment of silence and prayer. The results are worth it. For instead of feeling torn and distracted, we shall begin, in prayer, to sense ourselves as "coming together."

If you wish to come home to God, you must first come home to yourself. When your vision becomes clouded over with responsibilities and obligations, restore your peace by taking a walk under the stars, looking up, and spending a few moments in silence.

People need such an attitude of wonder, for it helps develop a true sense of proportion and distance. Wonder has a way of reducing us down to a joy-filled life size. We become less important to ourselves and more integral to the world around us which is filled with God's presence. Wonder lifts us out of ourselves. This is what the psalmist felt when he looked into the night sky and saw how vast it was and how small by comparison he was! Yet God loved him more than all the rest of creation:

Oh Lord! How wonderful you are.
Even though we only dimly sense this at
    times,
Still your presence fills the earth
And the heavens, too!
When I look up into the night skies
And see the work of your hands—
The moon and the stars which you have
    made—
My breath is taken away.
How could you be interested in us?
Why would you pay any attention to us?
But you do!
Yes! You have created us with an undying
    spirit, a mind and a heart that seek you
    out at every turn of life.
Our very search for you is your gift!

Oh, Lord God! The wonder of your
    presence fills the earth and echoes in
    our hearts.

Psalm 8 (paraphrased)

# FIVE

# *What You Give, You Get*

*Don't worry about anything, but in all your prayers ask God for what you need, always asking him with a thankful heart.*

Philippians 4:6

This is fine for Paul to say. After all, he was especially favored by God. It's easy to be thankful when you know that God is acting in and through you. And Paul knew that vividly. From that knowledge came all his letters to the Christians of his time. Whenever you pray, Paul is saying, go to God with thanksgiving. If you do that, you needn't worry.

Can thanksgiving be an abiding attitude? It depends upon what you are looking for. What you are looking for, *that* you will find, seems to be Paul's message. Approach God with a thankful heart and that is what you will find. What you give is what you get. That's one of the great spiritual laws: Love your neighbor *as* yourself.

Forgive us our sins *as* we forgive those who have sinned against us. Give love and you shall receive it. Give forgiveness and it shall be given to you. Aren't they all saying the same thing? What you give is what you get.

Another way of looking at it goes like this: What you receive, give away freely. Don't keep it. That way you confirm the gift within yourself.

Does this sound strange?


The servant in Matthew's gospel (18:23-35) was forgiven an enormous debt that he owed, but he didn't confirm the gift by giving that very grace away, so he lost it for himself. Right after being forgiven, he went out into the street and saw a man who owed him a few dollars. The servant started choking him—he wanted justice now! Mercy be damned! In such a small space of time he had forgotten.

So what he received as a gift, he lost because he didn't give it away. What you give is what you get in the spiritual life. That is why St. Paul says in his letter to go to God with a thankful heart. Go to him with a knowledge of all you have received—everything, really! Be grateful and you shall receive it.

But how can we be thankful when we have been touched by evil—and who hasn't? How can we be grateful when we are victims of injustice? That would seem to be the time to become anxious, distrustful! Yet, St. Paul, in his letter to the Philippians, wrote about not worrying and being thankful—while he was in prison. In chains. And his letter has been called the epistle of joy! He must have discovered a secret.

To get some insight into what that secret was we must ask what he was looking for.

*Live in union with him. Keep your roots deep in him, build your lives on him. . . . And be filled with thanksgiving.*

Colossians 2:6-7

To make things grow I must cherish and encourage every sign of life in others, forgetting their less-than-perfect performance for whatever is good in them. Otherwise, hope will never find a resting place in their hearts—or mine!

It is within my power to give someone hope!

What a startling thought! But why else are there differences among us? And what else shall I take out of life but what I give away, what I have passed on?

The gifts I have received are the coin to inspire hope and love in others. I lose nothing by generously giving praise and support to every attempt to achieve what is fine in life. It requires no lie from me to cherish what is good *for itself*—selecting this aspect of life, even looking for it—while at the same time overlooking what is less than perfect. This way I shall, in all things, be filled with thanksgiving.

*Jesus turned, saw them following him, and asked, "What are you looking for?"*

John 1:38

What you are looking for, that you will find.

Gilbert Keith Chesterton, an English essayist and novelist, spent 62 years looking for a way of thanking God for the great gift of life. If anything characterizes his writing, it is the optimism and gratitude he felt.

He never got over the delicious shock and wonder that he *did* exist—and didn't have to! How good of God to have thought of him, to have called him into existence. Never mind the failures. Never mind the social problems his generation faced—and to which he addressed himself. Never mind even death. He was alive!

Chesterton was looking for a way of expressing his thanks—a way of giving, not getting.

There was only one kind of person that Chesterton had little tolerance for: the pessimist, the kind of person who found fault with everything in life, finally rejecting the gift, along with the cosmos, as a hopelessly mixed-up puzzle. Taking the part of the offended cosmos, he wrote:

> A cosmos one day rebuked by a pessimist
> replied, "How can you who revile me consent to speak by my machinery? Permit
> me to reduce you to nothingness and then
> we will discuss the matter."
> Moral: You should never look a gift
> universe in the mouth.

God was the giver and he, Gilbert Keith Chesterton, the gift, which he enjoyed, along with all the others given him.

In another of his poems, he projects his own attitude into the thoughts of the child waiting to be born. The child promises anything—everything—to get the great gift of life:

> They should not hear from me a word of
>   selfishness or scorn
> If only I could find the door, if only I
>   were born.

It was inconceivable to Chesterton that the child would come into the world, then turn into a pessimist! That would be to go back on its promise. So it must, according to that promise, accept the world with all its puzzles, its contradictions and beauty—even the fact that it seems so fleeting.

For every objection the pessimist raised, Chesterton had a response.

"We are dust!" the skeptic said. "The whole of the earth merely a soap bubble. Life is fleeting."

Chesterton replied:

> Are we all dust? What a beautiful thing
> dust is, though. This round earth may be
> a soap bubble, but it must be admitted
> there are some pretty colors on it.

Chesterton refused to be negative, even in the face of pessimism:

What is the good of life? It is fleeting.
What good is a cup of coffee? It is fleeting.
Ha Ha Ha.

Chesterton's attitude was the opposite of care and
worry. It requires a lot of care, worry and anxiety to
maintain a name, security, importance, wealth, respect.
And once we get a small corner on some of these
things—once we are insured, so to speak—we are as like-
ly as not to look to *ourselves* in gratitude. Who achieved
it, after all?

At the point we begin to think *we* have earned it
all, we become rich in our own estimation; we forget
that all the gifts come from, and with, the first gift: life.
And that comes from God.

Scripture says, "Cast all your care on the Lord for
he cares for you."

To do so is the difference between thinking you
earned your own existence and knowing it is a gift. The
person who knows it is a gift and acts out of that
knowledge is a poor man, for he *has* cast all his care on
the Lord by his gratitude.

Chesterton was a poor man. He could trust God with the care of his life and still keep a contagious sense of humor.

Writing to his fiancee, Chesterton expressed in a poem his outlook on daily life:

Here dies another day
during which I have had eyes, ears, hands
and the great world around me
and tomorrow begins another.
Why am I allowed two?

Chesterton focused on the one thing necessary in life: gratitude for the gift of it. At the end of an intensely lived day, he was happy that he had that gift for even one day. Imagine having it for two! Because he was grateful, he could let go of the lesser things that make us feel important, privileged or secure—the things that swell the ego, making it feel self-sufficient, even independent of God.

In the gospel, poor persons are those who give up care and worry because in their hearts they believe that God cares for them. At that point a veil is lifted and they can begin to experience gratitude. It's worth considering that one of the things condemned by Christ in the parable of the sower and the seed (Mk 4:19), one of the things that prevents the coming of his kingdom within the heart, is worry and anxiety. They hinder gratitude: that spontaneous leap of the heart to its source.

# SIX

# Removing the Deserts

*There were so many people coming and going that Jesus and his disciples didn't even have time to eat. So he said to them, "Let us go off by ourselves to some place where we will be alone."*

Mark 6:31

Jesus spoke these words to his disciples right after the death of his friend John the Baptist. He felt the need to get away for a while.

Jesus was what you might call a high-profile person, so he had to consciously choose times of reflection and prayer. "Let us go off by ourselves," he said to his disciples, "where we will be alone and can rest awhile."

Where did he go? Into a desert, a lonely place of retreat where, with his friends, he could tap into the creative side of life. Only suddenly the lonely place wasn't so lonely! It was filled with people who knew where he was going. They wanted him to teach them and touch them. They were hungry and wanted to be fed by his word and presence. They, too, didn't have time to eat. And the Lord did teach them, heal their bodies and souls, and feed them. All in the desert! That is the place where these people experienced life. It seems contradictory, doesn't it, that it was in the desert that they met the Lord of Life?

Most people run from the experience of the desert in their lives. It seems empty even of God; a barren place where nothing can grow, one devoid of life, where we feel cut off, separated, alone.

There are many such deserts. These are the lonely places which few people see in us. It could be a physical or moral defect, the fact of aging, some recurring sickness. It might be a pattern of sin or some compulsive way of acting we can't seem to overcome. It's an experience of the desert when we feel like a personal failure or have a sense of being cheated in life. It could be a broken relationship in which we had hoped for so much that just never materialized. Any one of these things could be a wound that we carry with us—and sometimes never recover from! And then there is the final desert: death.

The desert is that within us which we would like to remove but can't. No medicine will heal it. No therapy take it away. And when we touch that desert place, it's as though we hear a voice cry out, "Failure! There is nothing here but failure and loss!" But could we make friends with the desert, could we listen compassionately, we might begin to hear another voice, faintly at first, barely audible. Listening makes it stronger, and here is what it says: "There is more to your life than what you see and feel, and even what you think."

Listening to that voice we shall be drawn to see more than the desert and the hold we have given it over us. Remember: The Lord is there in that defect, that fault or tragedy, *working* to take the very thing we reject and run from, to draw good out of it.

He teaches us and feeds us; heals us in the
desert—in that thing we are trying to get rid of—just as
he did to those who followed him. He doesn't remove
the desert, but brings into that empty waste his own
healing presence and eventual light.

*In all things God works for good with those who love him.*
Romans 8:28

There is no way that we can understand our lives
by looking only at the present moment. Looking
backward, we can sometimes pick up a "story line." Life
sometimes makes sense looking backward even though it
must be lived going forward. Some of the failures of the
past when looked at in light of the present might seem
radically different. At the time of a particular experience
we could see nothing good coming from it. Yet when
looked at in the light of what has happened, we might
see that it introduced a change, a new direction, and
our lives were enriched because of it.

The Hebrew people never forgot what the desert
meant for them. At the time of their experience it felt
like a misery. Yet looking back it was seen as the beginning of a new life with God. They saw that something
good came from what seemed only evil at the time. That
is why their poets wrote the following lines:

Let us thank Yahweh for his love,
for his marvels on behalf of men.
. . . he turned a desert into sheets of
water,

an arid country into flowing springs,
where he gave the hungry a home
in which to found a habitable town.

Psalm 107:31, 35-36 (JB)

God works for good with those who love him.
Notice that the verb in that sentence is "works," and
"God" is the subject. He is the one working in our lives
to bring about good. The *only* condition is that we love
him.

The things we endure, then, have a hidden potential, for he is at work turning what is negative and
destructive into what is *for* our good.

St. Paul, who wrote the above lines to the Romans,
learned in his own weakness to turn to God and rely
upon him, *not* upon himself—and he says this was the
hidden potential of his suffering. This and the ability to
touch others in their pain, to share grace with them, to
be able to heal because of what he had experienced. He
could bring relief to those who suffered similar pain and
weakness.

Dependence upon God, relying upon him, the ability to share with others, to touch and alleviate their
pain—all these are things one might see looking
backward. And these are the things, after all, that give
life meaning.

# SEVEN

# Living Now, Not Then

*"Console my people, console them. . . ."*
*Shout with a loud voice. . . .*
*"Here is your God." . . .*
*Do not be afraid, for I am with you;*
*stop being anxious and watchful, for I am your God.*
*I give you strength. I bring you help.*

Isaiah 40:1,9; 41:10 (JB)

Isaiah spoke these words for those who were seeking God but felt they had been abandoned by him. He says, "Fear not, *here* is your God."

Fear makes our minds race into the future as we desperately try to control our lives. Fear of the future constricts not only our minds, but our bodies as well. It distorts our perceptions and makes us judge others and ourselves in a half-light.

Fear makes us live everywhere else *but* here! And here, in this present moment, is where God is.

What discipline is required to live in the present moment—here! To draw back our imaginations and minds when they squander themselves trying to prophesy the future is difficult. Yet, we destroy our peace when we do not.

The source of our strength is in the present moment. And it is in this moment only that God is present to help us as Isaiah said. Where God is, there is the possibility of joy—the joy and strength of his presence.

Psalm 16 says of God that "because he is at my right hand (right now!), I shall not be moved. Therefore my heart is glad, and my soul rejoices." (RSV)

To live aware of this truth—that he is present to me now—is to let go of fear. Then will the promise of Isaiah to his people be realized: Streams will burst forth in the dry and hungry desert, ears shall hear melodies never before heard and the burning sands of doubt and fear shall become refreshing pools of water.

> "You are my servant,
> I have chosen you, not rejected you,"
> do not be afraid, for I am with you; . . .
> For I, Yahweh, your God,
> I am holding you by the right hand;
> I tell you, "Do not be afraid,
> I will help you." . . .
> I will make rivers well up on barren heights,
> and fountains in the midst of valleys;
> turn the wilderness into a lake,
> and dry ground into waterspring.
> In the wilderness I will put cedar trees,
> acacias, myrtles, olives.
> In the desert I will plant juniper,
> plane tree and cypress side by side.
>
> Isaiah 41:9-10,13,18-19 (JB)

*That is why I am going to block her way*
   *with thorns*
*and wall her in so that she cannot find*
   *her way;*
*she will chase after her lovers and never*
   *catch up with them,*
*she will search for them and never find*
   *them.*

*That is why I am going to lure her*
*and lead her out into the wilderness*
*and speak to her heart.*

Hosea 2:8-14 (JB)

Far from being a monolith in the sky, Hosea pictures the Lord as a jealous, passionate lover, one who hedges in his people, puts obstacles in her way, walling her up, and finally leading her out into the wilderness in order to get her quiet enough to speak to her heart! That kind of direction certainly gives a different way of looking at the events we live each day, in and through which God's providence reveals itself! It also says something about the way God looks at the potential in the wilderness, the thing we call a desert.

I will guide you. Not perhaps in the way you would like—but listen!

I am with you in every breath you draw, in each flash of beauty that enlightens your eyes.

I am with you, though your senses stand mute and unperceiving.

Believe in me, even in what you sense as danger. Believe!

Even though your heart speeds up and fear constricts your body, I am with you, in the center of your concern, for I love you. Rely on that always.

EIGHT

# If Your Heart Condemns You

*This is how our hearts will be confident in God's presence. If our conscience condemns us, we know that God is greater than our conscience and that he knows everything.*

1 John 3:19-20

Too often our hearts do not feel sure in God's presence because they condemn us—even when we are leading good lives and trying to serve God. At times like this the heart seems to become greater even than God! So John, knowing this much about the heart—that it *can* see nothing but itself when it is in the darkness—teaches that it still remains *our* heart, not God's. And God's is bigger, more understanding, more compassionate.

Our faith is in his heart, not our own.

We cannot determine whether God loves us from our feelings of being loved. Our feelings of being loved, after all, could be nothing more than pious self-enlargement, just as our awareness of being a sinner may well be an act of humility!

Nor can we look at one specific failing and let it swallow all the good we do daily.

We are called by God to live out our sometimes difficult personalities, attempting to turn volatile forces within us into a source of light for ourselves and others. In the process, because of the very complexity of divergent forces within us, we often fail. But it is a failure that comes from trying to do what is right, not what is wrong. No matter. God can and will save us, even as failures.

We have no other hope than to trust him with our—yes!—damnation! For we must trust all to him; and since we often feel we must earn what can't be earned, we must turn over to him even that which we want so badly: eternal life!

We try. Yet experience shows that we have not despotic control over our inner lives, only suasive. We look for a balance and work at it, too. Still our efforts are only tokens. The real balance between extremes comes from God working in and through life's events, both outer and inner, not simply from our will.

*"I am not worthy to have you come under my roof."*
Matthew 8:8 (RSV)

Lord Christ,
I wish I could offer you
a reasonably clean
and swept house
to dwell in,
but I can't.

I *can* say—and know the meaning of—
  "I am not worthy to have you come
  under my roof. . . ."
But you are already there!
Living among the once-flourishing idols.
The floor is dirty
and at times the room
is airless—
even for me!
I am ashamed of your presence there,
yet you slept in a cave
and on a donkey's back at night
under the desert stars.
So, if I can't change your
  accommodations,
let me rejoice all the same
that you are present.
I must believe strongly, Lord,
that I can't question this:
that you are at home
with sinners—
and my greatest sin, Lord Christ,
is that I don't want to be a sinner!
Nor do I easily accept it—still,
  the evidence
  is overwhelming.
But hope is like a green shoot
in the midst of an airless, disordered
  world.
And that hope comes from your Spirit.
I rest in that hope,
Lord.

This, then, is how we will know that we belong to the truth; this is how we will be confident in God's presence. If our conscience condemns us, we know that God is greater than our conscience and that he knows everything. And so, my dear friends, if our conscience does not condemn us, we have courage in God's presence.

1 John 3:19-21

Either way, we are called to have courage in God's presence.

# NINE

# The Three-Minute Mile

*"Lead us not into temptation, but deliver us from evil."*
Matthew 6:13 (RSV)

Does God tempt us? Does he lay in wait to catch us off guard?

Such a belief that God would tempt us to evil is unacceptable to the human mind and heart—and with good reason!

There are two meanings to the word "tempt": one, to draw someone to evil; the other, to test. This second meaning has nothing to do with evil. Rather, it is to challenge someone in such a way that what is deepest and most good will be revealed.

A runner attempts a three-minute mile and a student attempts graduate studies. Why? To achieve what is good—and what would not be achieved without attempting it.

One meaning of the word "tempt" is to draw someone to evil; the other, toward good. God never tempts a man or woman to evil. But he always challenges and tests them to achieve the greatest good.

*But even though he was God's son, he learned through his suffering to be obedient.*

Hebrews 5:8

The scriptures themselves say that Jesus learned obedience through suffering. That is, he was tested. When that is translated into 20th-century life, it means that he attempted to run his race of life in a broken world and succeeded, without becoming a rebel, and without retaliation. He was ready for life, even when it led to death—and he was rewarded with God's full acceptance of his offering, which we call resurrection.

The whole of life is a testing, an attempt.

And a good part of our suffering comes from looking at it as something final, as though *"If only* I could find the right combination, I would be permanently happy."

The "if onlys" and the illusion of permanent happiness in this world often cause needless suffering. They cause us to alternate between intolerable lows caused by our feelings of guilt—"there must have been something I could have done and didn't," "if only"—and unreal highs caused by our illusions of what life should be.

Out of the highs and lows grows a vacuum.

But once we take our eyes off the "if onlys" and the illusion of "permanent happiness" in this life right around the corner, once we begin to look at life as a series of challenges leading to a discovery of who we are, then the burden is lifted.

"Learn from me," Jesus said, "because I am gentle and humble in spirit." Take on my burden of living in this present moment and letting go of your illusions—which is far lighter than the one you carry—and you will at the same time find peace.

We, too, run our race in a broken world, but one in which there is much goodness. That goodness is revealed through testing which life itself manages to bring us.

God is in our struggles to bring about our growth and healing.

# TEN

# Making a God of Your Own

*Instead of worshiping the immortal God, they worship images.*

Romans 1:23

A close friend of God, Simone Weil, wrote in her journal that life is so intolerable for most men and women that they must invent false gods or illusions in order to get through just one week of it!

One of the illusions is the firmly held belief that the future is a place up ahead which is filled with all the good things we want now, but can't get. "The grass is greener on the other side," we say—any place, that is, except where we are or who we are!

"Somewhere over the rainbow," goes the song—somewhere up ahead is that place filled with all the good things we want. The problem with this belief is that it takes away the need to live here and now, in this city, with these people, with this personality.

That is the way of illusions. They distract us—drag us away—from living life now.

But God's grace and his presence is only perceived in this present moment, never in the future, since it never exists except as a "now."

*"Your father already knows what you need before you ask him."*

Matthew 6:8

Another false god or illusion that makes it tolerable for people to make it through the week is to confuse what we want with what we need.

Needs are quite simple: food, clothing, shelter, love, work and companionship, sleep.

But wants are desires over and above what we *need* to live. Once we say—and this is the illusion—that everything we want we *need*, then there is no end to our needs! And needs have to be fulfilled!

With this mentality we lose a sense of proportion and turn to constant consumption of everything and everyone to fill the growing vacuum within. We try to fill our empty hearts by consuming people and things. And there is no room left for the living God.

> But the most miserable people of all
> are those who rest their hopes on lifeless
>     things,
> who worship things that have been made
> by human hands—images of animals
>     artistically made
> from gold and silver,
> or some useless stone carved by someone
>     years ago.
> A skilled woodworker may saw down
>     some suitable tree,
> carefully strip off the bark,
> and then, with skilled craftsmanship . . .
>     carefully carve it

in his leisure time, using spare moments
to shape it into the crude image of a
  person,
or maybe of some worthless animal.
He paints it all over with red,
covering up every flaw in the work.
Then he prepares a suitable place in the
  wall for it
and fastens it in place with iron nails.
He is careful to keep it from falling,
because he knows it is only an idol
and needs help; it cannot help itself. . . .
It is weak, but he prays to it for health.
It is dead, but he prays to it for life.
It has no experience, but he prays to it for
  help.
It cannot walk, but he prays to it for a
  successful journey.
Its hands have no power
but he asks it to help him.

                    Wisdom 13:10-11,13-16,18-19

ELEVEN

# Letting Go

*When the man heard this, gloom spread over his face, and he went away sad, because he was very rich.*

Mark 10:22

Every Christian has heard the story of the rich young man who came up to Christ and asked him what he had to do to gain everlasting life. The Lord replied simply, "Keep the commandments." The young man said, "I have since I was a child."

Jesus was moved by the earnestness of the man and his desire to be good. Scripture says the Lord looked straight at him with love, then said, "You need only one thing. Go and sell all you have and give the money to the poor, and you will have riches in heaven; then, come and follow me."

When the young man heard this, gloom spread over his face and he went away sad, because he was very rich.

This story is not about money. If the Lord had asked the man for a thousand dollars, he would have written a check immediately. Nor is it a story about hoarding money.

Christ was asking a deeper question of the young man: Can you let go of all the worry, the concern and anxiety, the constant vigilance needed to maintain all the wealth you have?

That's what it means to become poor. Can you let go of all that concern about your own life and give it over to Christ?

St. Peter advised his friends to "leave all your worries with him, because he cares for you." One *must* be poor to follow Christ! We must finally let go of the anxiety and worry about our own life.

The rich man couldn't do this, so he went away sad. But who knows? All things are possible with God. Maybe after thinking it over, remembering that direct look of the Lord into his heart, maybe he came back to talk again with Jesus.

*But all those things that I might count as profit I now reckon as loss for Christ's sake.*

Philippians 3:7

Paul was a rich man, in a way. And sometimes his language seems to suggest that he had a good knowledge of business: profit, loss, reward. His wealth consisted in being born into the tribe of Benjamin. He had status from birth in his country. But not just that, he was educated by the best of teachers, and that is a form of

wealth. He led what he calls a righteous life, another form of wealth. He had the law and the prophets which he embodied. He traveled widely, saw the great cities of the ancient world, probably witnessed the Olympics, yet when weighing all of these advantages and trying to discern their worth, he said: "I reckon everything as complete loss for the sake of what is so much more valuable, the knowledge of Christ Jesus my Lord. For his sake I have thrown everything away; I consider it all as mere garbage, so that I might gain Christ, and be completely united with him."

He could let go of his life and turn it over to Christ so much so that he relied on the Lord's strength, present to him, on every occasion. Whether things were going well or not wasn't the point—what he learned about Christ was! He was the one who guaranteed his life and cared for him.

> I have learned to be satisfied with what I
>     have.
> I know what it is to be in need
> and what it is to have more than
>     enough.
> I have learned this secret,
> so that anywhere, at any time, I am
>     content,
> whether I am full or hungry,
> whether I have too much or too little.
> I have the strength to face all conditions
> by the power that Christ gives me.
>                         Philippians 4:11-13

# TWELVE

# Resurrecting the Buried Self

*"If anyone wants to come with me, he must forget himself, carry his cross, and follow me. For whoever wants to save his own life, will lose it; but whoever loses his life for my sake will find it. Will a man gain anything if he wins the whole world but loses his life?"*

Matthew 16:24-26

Notice that there are two "selves" that the Lord is talking about: one worth losing and one worth saving, a false self and a true self. And the true self is worth more than the whole world! That self is the proper self, the one that is buried—or better—only slowly emerging. Carrying the cross is all the work needed to help that true self emerge, which often means dealing directly with negative emotions of hatred, anger, fear—and that is work!

Negative emotions are behind all kinds of disorderly thinking, ways by which we disqualify what is good in ourselves or others. After a successful performance, for instance, someone congratulates us and we, with apparent humility, say, "Oh, it wasn't really anything." To function in this way we must look for the good thing, deny it, and live with the consequent negative emotion.

And we do the same for others too! "What is so good about what he did?" Negative! Disqualified good. Cancelled out. This is the false self at it subtlest. And the false self is condemned to death with the coming of the Light, Jesus Christ.

The problem of negative thoughts and emotions comes from looking at the world only in relation to oneself—and the self that loses out is the true self, the creative, compassionate, outgoing force within us.

If we could see the world as a gift, we would be less fearful; there would be less condemnation, less of the wrong kind of competition. It is when we forget that we are guests in the house and believe that we must build the house all by ourselves—competing with everyone else in the process—that we lose our peace. The trouble starts when we forget we are guests. Then the world becomes *our* world! And we become responsible for its continued existence. Ever so subtly our ego inflates like a gigantic circus balloon, a "comic-god" that demands the sacrifice of others—even our best self—to our compulsive needs.

This is how we wound ourselves, trying to save our own lives as we rush headlong into disaster to prove something to someone. Then comes the crash, the crisis, the disappointment, the disillusionment, and the time for the simple prayer of surrender.

All of this is a pattern, a process, by which we learn over and over what it means to be a child of God, turning over our distorted ideas of *being* God!

Where is this done—and how? In prayer.

People, places, talents of life are gifts—*not* possessions! They are best received by not laying hold on them.

Resentment, anger and hatred are the forces in creation that darken our minds and prevent us from seeing what is really present.

The desire to be better than the best, just to be even, is the cause of much anger. Surrender that and you'll know peace.

Have you wasted so much time and nervous effort trying to construct a future that would avoid failure and guarantee success that you have forgotten how to live in the present? And have you wasted even more time in blaming others, places, and things for your real or imagined failure that you distorted their true worth and your own in the process?

We wound ourselves! Yet God can and will heal us in prayer. Don't, however, ask him to deliver you from some evil or failure. Don't ask him to take away evil thoughts or fear of the future. So often this kind of prayer only conceals the need to succeed!

Far better to turn the thought, deed or situation over to Christ genuinely. He knows.

To do this is to relate yourself in all things to the Lord. Let him shape the success or failure in your life.

Lord, you know how much I want to see
    your kingdom come about—
at least I think I do,
though when people cross me
and I can't build my world the way I
    know is best,
I get angry.
And even plot revenge in my heart;
but first, Lord, I must entertain feelings of
    being wounded,
victimized,
unfairly treated—I carry all these thoughts
    around with me,
the useless lumber of fear, guilt and
    condemnation.
Hardly the material for a good foundation
    to build on. Sand, really!
And you said that if I build on sand
my house will perish: My true self will
    never emerge,
the self built on a rock. It's that self,
    Lord, that I wish to encourage:
the self that goes out to others in
    forgiveness
and compassion,
the self that is unconcerned with negative
    thoughts.
Help me, Lord, to see and live this way
in imitation of your son,
Jesus Christ.

# THIRTEEN

# Sharing Who We Are

*Let us love one another, because love comes from God.*
*Whoever loves is a child of God and knows God . . . for*
*God is love.*

1 John 4:7-8

No matter how deeply we can share our experiences with others and no matter how much we love and are loved in return, there is no way that we can share *all* of who we are. There is always a place where finally we are alone.

That sense of being alone, even in the midst of friends, can be devastating, as though no one really knows us. Worse—perhaps we don't even know ourselves!

Despite medicine and psychology, the study of the body and mind, we remain a mystery to ourselves. Our deepest experiences of life cannot be communicated. And that is where we feel our loneliness greatly.

What is this mystery of loneliness, of never seeming able to be fulfilled? Is it hunger? For no matter how much is given to us, we are still hungry for something more: something not within reach, not quite seen, but up ahead, which draws us on through life, looking, hoping.

To experience aloneness in this way is not a sign of sickness. It can come right in the midst of happiness! Rather, it is a sign of health, a direction toward the one who brought us into being.

Were we satisfied along the way, once and for all, it would show that we were not created for something greater than what we can see and feel.

Man was created by God for love. And God *is* love! All the fragmentary experiences of love that we have throughout life *hint* at this, so they can't satisfy our desire. They are conductors to bring us more surely to their source.

And does he really know us? More importantly, does he love us? Is he present to the hunger and ache that are often masked over and forgotten in everyday life? There is never a doubt about the answer to this question in the minds and thoughts of those who have come close to the mystery that God is. He is always present to us, most especially when we feel that keen sense of aloneness.

That is when God acts directly on the heart, drawing it out and beyond itself.

> My Lord! You know who I am.
> You know where I am
> And what I do.
> You see and love all that is about me.
> You know the words
> Formed in my heart
> And not yet on my tongue—
> Nor can I understand such a thing!
> It is too marvelous for me.
> You surround me, Lord, with your care,
> Shielding me with your hand.

I can't understand these things;
My mind can't grasp them!
Could I escape from you, Lord?
Where could I go?
If I were to soar into the heavens,
You would be there;
And if I flew to where the sun rises,
East across the sea,
Your hand would guide me!
Even if darkness were to cover me,
Concealing me from your sight—
What is darkness to you?

You are the one who gave me my inner
    self
When you put me together in my
    mother's womb.
For such a mystery, I thank you, Lord.

For the wonder that I am, I thank you!
For all of your creation, I thank you!

Oh Lord God! You do know me,
For you watched my bones taking shape
When I was being formed in secret,
Knitted together in my mother's womb.

My God! How hard it is to grasp your
    thoughts!
How impossible to understand
That you are at the center of my life
Drawing me toward you,
The love of my life.

                    Psalm 139 (paraphrased)

# FOURTEEN

# Making Up Your Mind

*As the time drew near when Jesus would be taken . . . he made up his mind and set out on his way to Jerusalem.*

Luke 9:51

Toward the end of his life Jesus realized that a conflict with the religious leaders of his time was inevitable. A collision course couldn't be avoided because of what he was teaching—the coming of God's kingdom, *his* justice—and because of the increasing number of people listening to and following him.

He had deep feelings about Jerusalem and its people—*his* people, after all. To them he was sent. And to them he wanted to proclaim God's mercy and love which would entail the conversion of the human heart. Just how strongly Jesus felt is echoed in Matthew's gospel: He looked upon the city and said, "How many times I wanted to put my arms around all your people!" What striking imagery! It revealed right away what his deepest motives were.

Because he wanted to put his arms around his people, he risked death to talk to them. Yet when he tried to explain this to his disciples, they got depressed. Scripture says of them that they became alarmed and became afraid when he told them what would happen were he to go into the city. Finally, perhaps impatiently, Jesus made up his mind. "Listen!" he told his disciples. "We are going up to Jerusalem." The thing that he wanted to do—and wanted to avoid—could be put off no longer. Luke says of Jesus that "he made up his mind and set out on his way to Jerusalem."

At this point he was alone, headed for certain disaster. His disciples and followers didn't understand. No one around him understood why he would choose to walk into the jaws of death, for that is all they could see coming from his decision.

How many hard decisions must be made in the same way for all of us!

We weigh the pros and cons; we talk to friends who can never really understand. We pray to God hoping to get some insight about what to do. And, finally, we are left alone, without a shelter it seems, bareheaded, in the dark, on the road to Jerusalem, doing what we must.

All we have left then is our life; instinctively we reach out to the source of life, and in that aloneness we touch something vital that gives us courage to go on walking.

O Lord, my God, you are my shelter.
You are the roof over my head!
My protector.
I run to you for safekeeping.
For you are my God;
And all the good things I have come from
    you.
And your people, Lord, how good they
    are!
It is a great pleasure to live with them.


Yet, you are all I have;
You give me all I need.
My future is in your hands.
When I look around and within me
How many are the gifts you have given
    me;
And how wonderful they are!
Because of them,
I am always aware of your presence.
You are near,
And nothing can shake me.
So I am filled with gladness
Since I know you will protect me.
The one you love,
You will not allow me to see the place of
    the dead.
No. Instead, you will show me the path
    that leads to life.
In your presence, Lord, I shall rejoice
    forever.

                Psalm 16 (paraphrased)

*In the fourth watch of the night he went toward them walk-
ing on the lake, and . . . they were terrified.*

Matthew 14:25-27 (JB)

The two disciples walking the road from Jerusalem
to Emmaus with their unknown Lord said as they
reached their home, "Stay with us; the day is almost
over and it is getting dark." Yet in the above incident
the disciples were terrified because of the Lord's appearance in the dark. His approach caused fear.

This incident is worth looking at and praying over
because it has a counterpart in the inner life of the
spirit. There are many important meetings of the Lord
in the dark! Jacob wrestled with the mysterious stranger
in the dark and came away wounded. Nicodemus came
to the Lord in the dark and came away converted. We,
too, meet him in the darkness, and often, like the
disciples rowing on the lake, when we have reached the
end of our strength, in the midst of a storm. Then we
become afraid at the unusual way the Lord comes to us,
using his own power which is quite different from the
kind of power we have exhausted.

It is hard to believe his words to us: "Courage! It is
I. Don't be afraid!" It seems like asking for the impossible since everything around and in us cries out danger
or deception. This is the beginning of the prayer of
faith.


*"I am the light of the world. Whoever follows me will have
the light of life and will never walk in the darkness."*

John 8:12

Yes, Lord, I do believe,
help me in my unbelief,
caused by my need to see
by my own light.
Help me in the unbelief
of needing to find my own way,
discover my own truth,
create my own life!
I'm really not much different from
    Thomas, Lord,
who wanted to do it all by himself
when he asked you to explain the Way
    to him,
and you surprised him with:
I am the way, I am the truth, I am the
    life.
That is what I wish to believe, Lord!
I want to shed my own darkness
and believe without seeing,
that you go ahead of me—and beside
    me—
within me, Christ!
If my darkness is a cover for your light,
    Lord,
let me walk in faith, confidently,
unafraid of the voices that tell me
    otherwise.
I want *you* to save me, Lord!
I can't save myself,
for I don't know the path I'm traveling
    on—you do.
I believe in that truth.

# FIFTEEN

# Seeing and Being Seen

*But Yahweh God called to the man. "Where are you?" he asked. "I heard the sound of you in the garden;" he replied, ". . . so I hid."*

Genesis 3:9-10 (JB)

There is a quality in prayer which, for lack of a better word, might be called transparency. Simply put, it means being honest and direct, not hiding from God no matter what the feeling or desire! For most of us this is very difficult because we are rarely honest with ourselves. So how can we be honest with God in whose eyes we want to appear our best?

This quality can be developed. God, after all, isn't away from us. Most especially he is within us at the very heart of life. There is no breathing without God, no seeing, no feeling, no loving! The mind and heart that read these words are sustained in existence by his life. He is the vital force that keeps us living. How easy it is to forget this fact.

When we attend a prayer service or a meeting and someone says, "Let us put ourselves into the presence of God," what that person is really saying is this: Let us remember, let us call to mind, a reality that is constant. We are constantly in the presence of God. There is no way we can escape!

The Jewish people at the time of Christ recognized that there was one exception to the law that forbade working on the Sabbath—only one: God could work on that day! For unless he worked, it would all cease to be.

We are always in the presence of God.

As St. Augustine said so well, "He is more intimate to me than my most intimate self." How then can we succeed in hiding from him? How can we escape his presence? Only by constructing illusions that block out this knowledge from our minds, and allow us to think we are god!

Transparency in prayer means moving through these illusions to the truth.

It means coming into vital contact with the living force within us and being honest about it: honest about ourselves, our likes and dislikes, our love and our anger—anger, even, with God. This is what a real honest dialogue is about. It is real prayer, and there is nothing dead about it at all. It's the kind of prayer God likes and listens to. It's the prayer of Jeremiah and Job; Adam should have tried it too!

Not to be honest in prayer is to construct the greatest of illusions and to cut oneself off from the source of life and strength.

Everyone must give up—but there are two ways of doing it: one, to give up *away* from life; the other, to give up *into* life. To give up *away* from life is suicide. But to pray and not be honest with God is to commit spiritual suicide. He already knows us thoroughly, so being honest in prayer finally means coming to know and accept oneself as a gift, along with the Giver. It's that simple. Give up, *into* life. There are times in life when everything seems to come undone. Our worlds collapse. Again, this is the time to give up *into* life, to hope beyond hope, and to take what has happened to him in honest, direct prayer. Pour out your heart's feelings. And when that is done, listen.

When in misfortune, pray out of misfortune, as the author of Psalm 102 did—an honest prayer filled with anguish and praise; the prayer of a man wondering how long he will live, and asking God not to forget him. God will listen to this kind of prayer for it is life calling out to Life to save it.

> Lord God, hear my prayer!
> Let my cry reach you.
> Don't hide now that I am in trouble—
> Listen to me!
> Be quick to answer me!
> For my days are vanishing like smoke,
>    my bones smouldering like logs,
>    my heart shriveling up like scorched
>    grass,
>    and my appetite has disappeared.

Whenever I breathe, my bones stick
through my skin.
I live in a desert,
in a ruin, like the screech owl.
I stay awake at night, crying out like a
lone bird on the rooftop.
Ashes are the bread I eat.
What I drink, I lace with tears.
It seems you only pick me up to throw me
down!
My days dwindle away like a shadow.
I am as dry as hay—
But you, Lord, you remain forever;
And man always remembers you!

Listen, Lord!
You promised to answer the prayer of the
abandoned;
You promised not to scorn their petitions.
Look down from the heavens,
And hear the sight of the captive.
Set free those doomed to die, as I am!
My strength has already run out;
Tell me, how much longer have I?
Do not take *me* prematurely,
When *your* life lasts forever!

Years beyond memory you laid earth's
foundations;
The heavens are the work of your
hands—
all will vanish!
All shall wear out like a garment,
like clothes that need changing—
but you yourself shall never change.
Your years are unending.
Give me life, then, and health!
Save me!

Psalm 102 (paraphrased)

Then Jesus went with his disciples to a place called Gethsemane, and he said to them, "Sit here while I go over there and pray." He took with him Peter and the two sons of Zebedee. Grief and anguish came over him, and he said to them, "The sorrow in my heart is so great that it almost crushes me. Stay here and keep watch with me."

He went a little farther on, threw himself face downward on the ground, and prayed, "My Father, if it is possible, take this cup of suffering from me! Yet not what I want, but what you want."

Once more, Jesus went away and prayed, "My Father, if this cup of suffering cannot be taken away unless I drink it, your will be done." He returned once more and found the disciples asleep; they could not keep their eyes open.

Again Jesus left them, went away, and prayed the third time, saying the same words.

Matthew 26:36-44

# SIXTEEN

# The Eyes Have It

*The Lord turned around and looked straight at Peter, and Peter remembered that the Lord had said to him, "Before the rooster crows tonight, you will say three times that you do not know me." Peter went out and wept bitterly.*

Luke 22:61-62

Very few times is it mentioned in scripture that Jesus looked *directly* at someone. But when it is said, it always involves a response on the part of the person Jesus looks at—a marked response!

When he healed the man with the crippled hand, he first asked the keepers of the law if he was allowed to heal on the Sabbath. Since there was no response, "Jesus was angry as he looked around at them, but at the same time he felt sorry for them" (Mk 3:5-6). Then he healed the man, after which "they" went outside and plotted his death.

In that look they were seen. So, too, their duplicity. Yet the look was not one of condemnation; not when it says he felt sorry for them.

When Jesus was walking beneath the sycamore tree, apparently oblivious to Zacchaeus in its branches, who would have guessed that he would have noticed this sinner? And scripture says, "he looked up and said to Zacchaeus, 'Hurry down, Zacchaeus, because I must stay in your house today.'" Again the marked response to the direct look of Jesus: Zacchaeus becomes a disciple. His life is changed by that direct look.

About the rich man Jesus met on the road—the one who wanted to follow him—Mark says, "Jesus looked straight at him with love." And the rich man's face fell. He became sad and walked away. But again, the look of Jesus was not one of condemnation. It never is—though it often provokes a crisis, a time of judgment. The judgment, however, is always an invitation, one made as scripture says, from love.

During the betrayal the Lord looked *straight* at Peter at the very moment he was immersed in his denial. Peter himself even believed what he was saying and that was the tragedy. He had wrapped himself in the icy calm of denial, and the Lord's look shattered Peter's composure. More importantly, it broke through his self-hatred, for Peter had denied the one person he loved above all loves. To persist in that denial, he would have had to do violence to everything sensitive in himself.

Christ's look went straight to the heart of Peter. In that moment he was converted. That was the beginning of his reconciliation. And fittingly, the cock crowed, for it was the beginning of dawn for him.

The crisis or judgment for Peter was Christ's love. How painful! But it opened Peter up to the deeper truth buried in his heart, the one he was denying. Pain? Yes, but the ice broke, for Peter went outside and wept bitterly.

We need never fear Christ's condemnation. The danger is not that God condemns or hates us, but that we hate ourselves and stay trapped in that guilt and hatred. Walled in! The crisis comes when the wall comes apart and we are seen by the Lord, but it's a crisis that leads to healing.

SEVENTEEN

# The Pain of Desire

*We want to remind you, brothers, of the trouble we had in the province of Asia. The burdens laid upon us were so great and so heavy that we gave up all hope of staying alive . . . . But this happened so that we should rely, not upon ourselves, but only on God, who raises the dead.*

2 Corinthians 1:8,9

Suffering is inevitable if one is longing for what is most deeply true about life. In fact, it is something released by desire itself, its very nature! When we cease to desire, we stop suffering.

The Greeks called that state "apathy," the inability to suffer.

Scripture says that the invisibleness of God is made visible by our talents, our gifts and our calling. But something far more mysterious about God is made visible in suffering. Again, this has to do with desire—God's desire! Love, especially the love of God, is a wound, a suffering, and for the same reason, desire.

Suffering—when it can't be avoided and is accepted—leads us to become more sensitive to the hurt in others. It allows us to sense that hurt and lay a healing hand on it, for grace is, through suffering, passed *through* our hearts *for* others.

Suffering not only opens up an inner way with others, it also leads us to rely upon God. This is especially true of the suffering caused by the desire for what is right, just, true—from which God often seems to be absent. Perhaps his presence is other than we realize!

Perhaps it is *in* that very desire!

The question of where suffering comes from cannot be answered except by reflecting on the nature of desire. A question that leads nowhere is to ask if God desires suffering. Better to ask, "Does God desire?"

> When the hour came he took his place at table, and the apostles with him. And he said to them, "I have longed to eat this passover with you before I suffer; because I tell you, I shall not eat it again until it is fulfilled in the kingdom of God."
> Then taking a cup, he gave thanks and said, "Take this and share it among you, because from now on, I tell you, I shall not drink wine until the kingdom of God comes."
> Then he took some bread, and when he had given thanks, broke it and gave it to them saying, "This is my body which will be given for you; do this as a memorial of me." He did the same with the cup after supper, and said, "This cup is the new covenant in my blood which will be poured out for you."
>
> Luke 22:14-20 (JB)

God's desire! He *longed* to mix his blood with ours. Even to break his body in our service, in ministering to us who are wounded. But these words above stand for us too. It is desire, after all, that leads us into communion with Christ; suffering desire that breaks its body and pours out its blood for others.

73

To realize how tightly our desire has bonded us to Christ, say the words of consecration over in your mind with the realization that you are promising your body and blood to others. That is the other half of the communion equation.

The Eucharist—communion—makes no sense whatever, except in the context of desire. To give in this way, totally, is to suffer for the one you love.

# EIGHTEEN

# God-thoughts

*"The Son of Man must suffer much. . . . He will be put to death, but three days later he will rise to life." He made this very clear to them.*

Mark 8:31-32

The Lord was walking with his disciples away from the Lake of Galilee toward the villages north. On the way he turned to them and asked what may seem to be a strange question: "Tell me, who do people say I am?" He got some mixed answers from his followers who were reporting what others thought about him: that he was John the Baptist come back from the dead or that he was Elijah the prophet who was supposed to return to earth to prepare the way for the Messiah. Others said he was simply a great prophet. Jesus then asked his disciples, "Who do you say I am?"

That question was a little closer to home and must have caught his disciples off balance—but not Peter! He immediately came up with the right answer: "You are the Messiah."

Peter was nothing but confident. And the Lord congratulated him for he had brought forth a "God-thought," a gift from God that he had welcomed. Otherwise he never could have said what he did. Just how far off Peter *was* in understanding what a Messiah was, however, becomes clear from what followed. Jesus impressed on their minds that he had to suffer much, be rejected by the very authorities they looked up to, be put to death, and after three days be raised to life.

Imagine the effect the Lord's words had on the disciples! You get some idea of their impact from what Peter did right after he heard them: He took Christ aside and began to rebuke him.

Reading and thinking of this now, we might wonder why he did such a thing; and why, too, it provoked such a strong reaction from the Lord. For he turned on Peter—remember, he had just praised him for having a "God-thought"—and called him a devil, telling him to get away from him. His thoughts *now* were "men's thoughts," not God's. There's a difference.

What's going on here? Why the sudden and deep flare-up from Jesus?

Look at the dynamic at work between Jesus and his disciples. They loved him, enjoyed being with him, had followed him with their lives—and now he is saying it is all over. Up ahead is suffering, rejection and death. That is what they heard—that is all they could hear!—suffering and death. The part about rising didn't register, couldn't register since they had not accepted death as a reality. How then could they understand resurrection? Neither could they understand the holding power of love. The two are tied together. There is no understanding one without the other.

Listen to a possible monologue that went on in Peter's mind after the Lord said he would have to suffer, die, and . . . and what? Peter speaks within, but his thoughts are directed to the Lord:

76

"I hear you. I know that you are saying it will all end: the sense of purpose and meaning in life; the joy we knew together in friendship, in being called; the good talks we had; the days when we fished and talked of the kingdom; the working together—the relationship with you which made all this possible, gave it meaning—*the* meaning in my life. All of it will stop! It will be ended in suffering, rejection, death! Don't say that! Don't even think that way! It's a temptation from the devil. Death ends love, so don't talk about death. Let us live now and forget about the future; forget about death."

Now imagine Christ speaking in reply:

"Yes, I am the Messiah, Peter, with death, rejection and resurrection on my mind—and in my destiny too— compelled to show you that love is stronger than death. I, too, have loved you and I have enjoyed sharing together, but that which drew and held us together is more powerful than death itself, more powerful than all of the power in the world. To show you this—to prove it—I must strip myself of all things and undergo the loss of everything, even this life of mine. Then I shall return to carry on this relationship which is stronger and more powerful than death. It is more lasting than anything in the world—everlasting. And I want you to be with me, Peter, but you must rid yourself of the idea that death is stronger than love. Peter, can you hear me? Are you listening? Follow me, Peter. Follow me."

# NINETEEN

# Just Passing Through

*"There are many rooms in my Father's house, and I am going to prepare a place for you. I would not tell you this if it were not so. And after I go and prepare a place for you, I will come back and take you to myself, so that you will be where I am."*

John 14:2-3

At the Last Supper, Jesus tried repeatedly to convince his friends that death was not terminal but a transition. He did so by speaking of the love he had for them that would last beyond death. He told them he must go, but that he would return in a deeper way. "Love and life will last," he said, as he picked up bread and wine to offer communion with them—a promise they didn't understand until after his death and rising. "Take and eat. By doing so, you live the endless, creative life that I do, flowing from my father."

The fear at the heart of all love is that of separation from those we love. Jesus says, "Never! That will not happen. Enter this abiding union with me over which death itself has no power."

Christianity is about relationships; not about temporary ones either, but those that last and which are imbedded in the Eucharist—in the heart of Christ. St. Paul says, ". . . from which they flow and in which they are brought to perfection."

Christ pioneered death, not by denial, but by admitting its existence and *passing through* it. The emphasis is on the words "passing through." Death is a transition. Just as the baby within the mother must die to that existence, literally be cut off from it, in order to see "mother" and grow in freedom and love, so with us.

And this is what Christ is teaching. We shall be cut loose from this life as he was in order to see and grow to perfection in our love for God and one another. In death we are not terminated. That is the message of the resurrection. Like Jesus, we shall pass through death to life without end, a life characterized by what God is: love.

The resurrection of Jesus is the showing of the Father's attitude toward us: wholly positive. Life!—creative and personal—above all, more deeply connected with those he loves, whom he goes out of his way to surprise and assure. They can hardly believe it! Nor can we!

The idea of the resurrection so attracts us that we are reluctant to believe. Is it easier to believe that death is terminal?

Will you tell me, Christ,
that all that is good shall be saved,
rescued,
carried over into new life?
Will the young girl with cancer,
bones hardly held together with
    skin—gaunt,
like a victim in a concentration
    camp—will she be saved, Lord?
Will she live again with new life?
And what of the young man
behind the wheel in a crushed automobile
with the motor on his lap—will he pass
    through death
into life, Lord?
I so want to believe
but the evidence to the contrary seems
    overwhelming, Christ!
Had I not your word,
and an inner conviction,
I could never believe that what is
    destroyed here
will rise to new life;
yet my life is based on this promise.


Someone will ask, "How can the dead
be raised to life? What kind of body will
they have?" You fool! When you plant a
seed in the ground it does not sprout to
life unless it dies. And what you plant is a
bare seed, perhaps a grain of wheat or
some other grain, not the full-bodied
plant that will later grow up.

                    1 Corinthians 15:35-37

This is how it will be when the dead are
raised to life. When the body is buried, it
is mortal; when raised, it will be immortal.
When buried, it is ugly and weak; when
raised, it will be beautiful and strong.
When buried, it is a physical body; when
raised, it will be a spiritual body.

1 Corinthians 15:42-44

# TWENTY

# Looking for the Way

*Thomas said to him, "Lord, we do not know where you are going; so how can we know the way?"*

John 14:5

The Lord had just told his disciples that he wanted them where he himself was. And he added, "You know how to get to the place where I am going." Thomas thought Jesus was talking about geography, so he was confused—just as we often become in trying to arrive at satisfactory decisions about life: Where should I go? Which one should I do? Should I stay with him or leave him? Should I change my job? Get married? What should I do? These are questions that come up frequently during a lifetime.

All these questions—and all others—get down to one question: What is the way, and how do I find it and take it? Jesus' answer to Thomas is this: The question about life is not about geography, it's about a person.

Jesus is the way and the going, the truth and the knowing, the life and the living. And, finally, life is not so much about what we *do*. It's about our relationship with Jesus Christ.

Peter discovered this painfully. You might say he

rediscovered it repeatedly after each fall. He avoided being lost by that discovery. When Peter was rebuked by the Lord for denying he would have to suffer, he was confronted with a choice: his own idea of what Jesus would be doing versus Jesus'. Not an easy choice, but one we must all eventually make. Peter could have walked off in a huff, as maybe Judas did, disappointed in Jesus. But he didn't. He made a choice: Jesus over his own idea. Not Peter's way, but the Lord's.

Again, at the washing of the feet, Peter was confronted with his way versus the Lord's. Peter knew for certain that the Lord should have nothing to do with serving his disciples. There was a lot of arrogance and manipulation hidden in Peter's seemingly humble exclamation: "You will never at any time wash my feet!" For Peter knew that power was given to rule, which was not the way with Jesus who said it was to serve. Once again a conflict situation: Whose way? Peter backed down when the Lord told him, "If I do not wash your feet, you will no longer be my disciple."

A choice for Peter! Whose way shall he follow? To Peter's credit—and he showed his bottom-line spirituality when he said it—"Lord, do not wash only my feet, then! Wash my head and hands, too!"

The way is a person, not an amassing of power concealed behind an empty ritual.

In the betrayal, Peter was locked into his own guilt and fear—and they make impenetrable walls! But when the Lord looked at him, something thawed inside Peter. He broke down and wept like a child, freed to make another choice of the way, Christ's way, over his own. To make that choice he had to give up ideas about his own strength and loyalty, ideas touching even on his manhood. He had to choose Christ over self-hatred, guilt and fear. Once again he chose Christ's way. And Christ's way is not that of self-hatred and guilt, which are too often disguised efforts at self-justification.

Finally, Peter was confronted with another, deeper decision. To make this one, he had to let go of all securities. It was either that, or lose Christ.

After the resurrection, when everything was all right between him and the Lord, Peter lost his balance and became worried about how close John was to Jesus, whether John would be free from death! And the Lord said, "What difference does it make to you? Follow me."

A choice again. A choice this time that meant leaving behind all ideas of who was "first," along with leaving behind even life itself!

We are all faced with similar choices as it becomes clear how radical a decision it is to follow Jesus Christ. He is to be preferred to all things! Yet we don't bring about the choosing situation. It's not as though, by our small acts of self-denial, we provoke a situation like that of Peter when his feet were being washed. It's the Lord's work. Still, we must make the choice: Christ over security, Christ over fear, Christ over success, Christ over failure.

How easy it is to settle down with the comforting belief that we have failed! There is even a certain satisfaction in it. We have tried and failed; we no longer exert any effort. All future activity will be specified by criticizing those who do!

Christ over—instead of—failure! Christ instead of death!

84

Christ is the way, and, as Thomas Aquinas said, we often limp along the way. Still, limping along the way is better than running full speed in some other way—our own!

The answer to the way is a person—a fact we clearly see when we're in love. Then the way seems clear. For a moment it seems that our way and *the* Way coincide. Until that vision is given to us, though, we move forward in faith. There is no possibility of going astray when our faith is in the person of Jesus Christ.

> "This is the way, walk in it," remarks Augustine. Walk by the way of the man Christ, and you will come to God. It is better to limp along the true way than to walk fearlessly apart from it. A man may limp along the true way and seem to advance little. Yet he does draw near the goal; but all the tireless running on the wrong road only takes one ever farther from the goal.
>
> If you are looking for your goal, cling to Christ. . . . Cling to Christ, then, if you want to be safe; you cannot go astray, for he is the way. Those who cling to him do not walk in pathless places, but along the straight road.
>
> St. Thomas Aquinas

What makes us continue living when we encounter overwhelming suffering? Why go on, except that we have a "gut feeling"—not a reasoned thought—about the goodness of life, despite the pain and obstacles?

When depressed, the imagination colors everything. Yet even in the midst of pain and fear, that inner feeling that I must walk forward and that this pain *will* end is present. Later, when the feelings have come up from their depressed cellar, I suddenly see and feel and know that life is to be lived and that it is good. My life, just as it is. When that happens, it's as though what held on during the depression or the pain inexplainably flowered and spread into my whole life, my mind, my spirit. I become the opposite of depressed: alive, creative, spontaneous.

It's because of these moments that we sense that life really does have a meaning for us, and one, through us, for others. When we string all these moments together, we see something of the story, our own story.

No amount of sickness, depression or failure that we have experienced is as strong as that story. When we see that much, we begin to get a clearer idea of what that "gut feeling" is that kept us going: the presence of God within, leading us on, telling us, "OK, now hang on for this one. Don't quit. Move beyond this obstacle. Keep walking and seek out the light. Be quiet and peaceful. There!—up ahead—there's a turn in the road and you'll see. Keep walking. I'm right here with you. Rely on that. Look for me there."

# TWENTY-ONE

# Judgment: Now and Forever

*"So then, if you are bringing your offering to the altar and there remember that your brother has something against you, leave your offering there before the altar, go and be reconciled with your brother first, and then come back and present your offering."*

Matthew 5:23-24 (JB)

If someone has wronged us and knows it, but does not have the humility to ask our forgiveness, yet all the time condemns himself or herself inwardly for the failure and breakdown in communication, then *we* are put into the reconciliation position. And if we act offended or hurt, using silence or distance to keep the offense before the person's eyes, then we become the one who is offending, because we know that by maintaining silence we confirm the bad opinion the other person has of himself or herself. We assent to the condemning judgment and in doing so, we punish that person further. This is a way of "fixing" the fault, a way of defining him or her by that failure. It is the opposite of reconciliation.

Notice now who should forgive! The tables have turned. Every crime or wound involves the consent of at least two people. So, too, does reconciliation. The question the wronged person must ask is, "Do I want the other person to go around with this rotten opinion of himself or herself? And do I want, by my action, to confirm that opinion?"

If so, why?

*And Jesus concluded, "So those who are last will be first, and those who are first will be last."*

Matthew 20:16

Swiss playwright Friedrich Duerrenmatt portrays the final judgment in a way consonant with the Lord's paradoxical statement of what the kingdom of God is like.

It is early morning. The sun is shining and many people dressed in long, white flowing robes are standing expectantly before two great closed doors. They are excited and happy for the doors into paradise which tower over them will soon be opened.

These are the people who have made it! And they are about to be rewarded. There is laughter and happiness in the crowd as people recognize and congratulate one another for having made it.

In the middle of this happiness a sound of static is heard coming from two great loudspeakers mounted high above the people. The static increases.

Obviously the switch has been turned on and someone is going to speak. The crowd becomes silent in anticipation. From the speakers comes the sound of a deep voice. Gabriel is speaking: "Attention! Attention! The Lord God has decided to forgive them all."

Stunned silence! Disbelief! Then low murmuring, gradually becoming louder, as the injustice of it sweeps through the crowd. How could he do such a thing? After the good lives *they* had led, he was letting them *all* in! Incredible! Disgraceful! Unjust! And at that moment, the sound of bugles comes from the loudspeakers: loud, sharp and clear. The last judgment had taken place at that moment.

# TWENTY-TWO

# God, a Learning Experience

*"Because I live, you also will live. . . . You are in me, just as I am in you."*

John 14:19-20

It's an error to think of God as being *only* outside, external to—and usually *above*—us. God, the mysterious presence of "the other," is deep within us, and this is what the Presence has revealed about himself: that he is within.

God is not competitive. He is not trying to snap us into line. He is not waiting for us to really mess things up so he can say, "See? I told you!"—and reject us. God *is* love. He doesn't play at it, as we do sometimes. He is that affirming presence which we sense in our quiet moments: looking at a child or being filled with wonder at a blazing sunset.

What does he want deep within us? He asks that we turn gently, quietly, yet firmly to him and have a wordless conversation. We depend on him for our being. He does not depend upon us for his being, yet he has made known who he is and where he lives. Why? It really comes down to this: He has *asked* for communion with us, for our love, which means we can refuse. We can refuse him something he desires—or something to which he has made himself vulnerable. The irony is that our very breath, our breathing, our spirits, are forever intertwined with God's, for we flow from him at this very moment. And that is the source of all true confidence.

We live because God wanted a conversation, a dialogue, a relationship with us. He spoke a word that is the same word we are known by: our name.

God is not much concerned with our failures—*we are*! He isn't concerned because he sees the whole of life as a learning experience. Failures to him are only like those of the small child crawling and stumbling—sometimes falling—in an attempt to walk. God looks at the walking, as we do when raising children. We don't correct the child for making a mistake when he or she is trying to do a good thing: learning to walk!

And even if we did, God doesn't.


*"What do you have that you did not receive? And if you did receive it, why do you boast as though you did not?"*
1 Corinthians 4:7 (NIV)


Because of education, the world we live in, and a tendency to distort the real meaning of Christianity, we conceal from ourselves the fact that all—everything that touches our lives—is a gift. In dry-eyed fatigue, we try to *earn* our existence and justify ourselves. We attempt (always unsuccessfully) to make over our world, and so we are always vaguely dissatisfied, often guilty, and sometimes even panic-stricken—for we are attempting the impossible.

When we do this, we are looking at the self as the center and source of all action and value. This is called idolatry, and the idol worshiper can only see God as an abstraction far beyond us, even opposed to us, as though he were playing with us like puppets on a string. Then we begin to fear not just life, but the Giver of life, who—in our fear-ridden minds—can prevent us from getting what we think necessary for our well-being! Or we tend to look at him as all-powerful, but mean, because he could help us, but does not. At this point, God becomes *externalized,* distorted.

The true God breathes compassionately at the very heart of our life and experience. And when we are distorted with fear, we must go and look at our deepest, most love-filled experiences: the quiet, treasure-filled moments when we sensed "the Other" present.

Recalling these experiences by memory is to recognize a little more clearly the mystery now present within us, now quietly at work—not as an alien force, an invader, but as a close, intimate guest with whom we can live without always talking to or taking care of. God is so close, so intimate, that we can forget him and he is not offended. Good friends can do that and live together, be together—and for long periods of silence, too.

# TWENTY-THREE

# Light in the Darkness

*"I am the light of the world. Whoever follows me will have the light of life and will never walk in darkness."*

John 8:12

It's a truism to say that good news *doesn't* sell; bad news *does*! Proof of that is the front page of the daily newspaper.

Given enough bad news, people get depressed and overcome with a feeling of helplessness, even paralysis, and finally darkness. Still, there is a circle of light in the darkness, and the Christian must continually return to that circle in order to be energized by it. In possession of that light, we can push back the darkness. With that light, we can bear and even overcome grief, sickness and death itself. That is the Good News.

And the Good News is a person, a circle of light in the darkness: Jesus Christ, present and in the most unlikely places!

A priest walked down a hospital corridor in the children's ward. He was young, just ordained. He stepped into a glassed-in room where an 11-year-old girl was lying in bed, paralyzed. Her arms were by her side. She was thin, eyes sunken but open. She saw nothing, though, for she was blind.

The priest was overwhelmed with a sense of helplessness, thinking of the prisoner inside the girl's body, locked in pain. Then he noticed that she and her mother had worked out a simple method of communication. If the girl moved her eyelid, that signified "yes." A move of the small finger on her right hand meant "no." No other parts of her body would move; only the eyelid and the small finger. Yes and no—and darkness and pain.

The priest imagined her pain, and would have liked to somehow reach inside her and remove it; bring some light into her darkness, if possible. But how? He leaned over the bed railing and spoke into the girl's ear. "Judy, can you hear me?" There was a slight movement of the girl's eyelid. "Yes." Then the priest, realizing he too could communicate with the girl, told her a story of color and action, a story of Jesus Christ as he walked over the yellow fields of Nazareth down toward the blue lake of Galilee. He spoke to her of the birds flying high in the air, the crowds at the water's edge, the boats and the smell of freshly caught fish—and of how Jesus loved everyone with all his heart. "Do you understand, Judy?" Again the flutter of the eyelid. "Yes."

The priest continued to tell the girl stories, day after day, as she grew more feeble. One day he asked her, "You hurt a lot inside, don't you, Judy?" The answer, "Yes." "Do you know that our Lord loved children in a special way?" The eyelid moved. "Do you know that he loves *you* in a very special way, Judy?" There was a pause, and then the eyelid moved again. Yes, she knew that!

Surrounded by darkness, rooted in pain, unable to move, Judy knew that Jesus Christ loved her!

94

All of the nurses working on that floor knew it too. The priest bent over and kissed the girl. There was so much light in the darkness!—a light stronger than sickness and paralysis, stronger than fear and death itself!

The LORD is my shepherd.
   I have everything I need.
He lets me rest in fields of green grass
   and leads me to quiet pools of fresh
      water.
He gives me new strength.
He guides me in the right paths,
   as he has promised.
Even if I go through the deepest darkness.
   I will not be afraid, LORD,
   for you are with me.
Your shepherd's rod and staff protect me.
You prepare a banquet for me.
   where all my enemies can see me;
you welcome me as an honored guest
   and fill my cup to the brim.
I know that your goodness and love will
     be with me all my life;
   and your house will be my home as
     long as I live.

                    Psalm 23

# TWENTY-FOUR

# How Much Are You Worth?

*"For you did not receive a spirit that makes you a slave again to fear, but you received the Spirit who makes you sons. . . . The Spirit helps us in our weakness. We do not know how we ought to pray, but the Spirit himself intercedes for us."*

Romans 8:15, 26 (NIV)

## The Spirit Intercedes

"It is because I love you that you are worth so much. That is why the Son said: 'Love your neighbor *as* you love yourself.' Did you notice that 'as'? Too often you forget it. It's very important. Without that 'as,' you would not do much in the way of love. What is it that makes you so valuable?

"There is no one like you. You are unique. My gift to you *is* you. You needn't create yourself. You needn't keep your world together. So turn to me, deep within, without anxiety and worry. Trust in me, for I have deep faith in you. I do trust in you. How do I make that clear?

"I don't care about your mistakes. I care about you. When you learn that, you will have learned that you needn't justify your existence. Depend on me even though it seems foolish to you—risky. Even when you don't believe that I am present to you or concerned with you; still, depend upon me and act. I will not give you a blueprint of your life, but I will be present to you in all your loving, compassion-filled experiences, and those that are filled with beauty. I will be with you. That is my promise. Can you risk such an act of confidence and trust?

"Don't fear! The disciples in the boat where Jesus was sleeping were terrified of the waves and his seeming unconcern, so they woke him up. I am awake! I am here! Risk your life by depending on me, *cheerfully*! I am in that risk."

# TWENTY-FIVE

# Bridges Are for Walking

*It is all God's work. It was God who reconciled us to himself through Christ and gave us the work of handing on this reconciliation. In other words, God in Christ was reconciling the world to himself.*

2 Corinthians 5:18-19 (JB)

Christ was the reconciler, a bridge joining two opposite sides together—God and us—and he got stepped on, too!

The price for bringing peace between us and God was the violence he accepted in this work of love.

We need bridges! We need them between races, between the young and the old, parents and children, between nations poised on the brink of destruction.

Most people know automatically how *not* to be a bridge. Demand an apology after a fight by sulking. Punish others by silence. In a warm-up argument, don't

listen but get your own arguments ready while the other person is talking. Use names that make people small; or use generalizations such as "All you men think alike," "You kids always look for the easy way out!"

How to be a bridge! Christ came to teach us how to be a reconciler, one who brings peace in the midst of conflict. We need bridges today as a way of solving our problems without hatred and violence.

*It is all God's work. It was God who reconciled us to himself through Christ and gave us the work of handing on this reconciliation.*

2 Corinthians 5:18 (JB)

## A Prayer of Reconciliation

Lord Christ, help us to see what it is that joins us together, not what separates us. For when we see only what it is that makes us different we too often become aware of what is wrong with others. We see only their faults and weaknesses, interpreting their actions as flowing from malice or hatred rather than fear. Even when confronted with evil, Lord, you forgave and sacrificed yourself rather than seek revenge. Teach us to do the same by the power of your Spirit.

TWENTY-SIX

# You Imitate the God You Believe In

*"I persecuted to the death the people who followed this way."*

Acts 22:4

You imitate the God you believe in.

Paul, before his conversion, believed in a destroyer-God—and he imitated him too. He protected his religion from those he thought would destroy it, those *outside* his religion. We call those outsiders Christians today.

The outsiders were the ones Paul hunted down, got evidence about and went into foreign cities to arrest, dragging them back in chains. He imprisoned, condemned and helped to kill them—all in the name of God!

Paul believed in a destroyer-God.

His conversion to Christ changed all that, for it was an experience of the Lord in the very people he was persecuting. That took some time to digest, for it meant a different way of looking upon the outsiders, whoever they were. To look through Christ's eyes is to see what is most good about people, what is most valuable in them.

*After* his conversion, Paul believed in a different God, a *saving* God. Instead of destroying others for God's sake, he turned toward saving them for God's sake.

In doing this, he was following in the way of the Lord Jesus Christ who didn't believe in a destroyer-God at all.

Follow the way of love, for that's the path that leads somewhere—to eternal life.

Paul understood this *after* his conversion.

## A God to believe in

> I believe in a God who constantly renews
>     my inner life, day by day,
> leading me to a deeper knowledge of him.
> I believe in a God who calls all men and
>     women to him out of a desire to share
>     what is most alive;
> a God who does not believe in nor want
>     injustice of any kind.
> I believe in a God who loves, always, all
>     that he has created,
> and has chosen each person to stand forth
> and become like him, through his Son,
>     Jesus Christ.
> I believe in a God of compassion, not
>     threats and revenge;
> one who seeks to find among his children
>     kindness
> and gentleness; above all, patience—that
>     long-suffering virtue!
> Above all, I believe in a God who forgives
> and gives new life,
> a God of new beginnings when only the
>     end seems a possibility.

I believe in the creative God, the artist
who drew all beings forth from chaos,
and loving what he saw, said: "It is
good!"
I believe in the God of relationships, who
calls people to one another—and
through that call to himself.
I believe in a God of peace who brings
people and nature itself together in
community with his Son.
I believe in the God of Jesus Christ whose
Spirit dwells within our hearts.

cf. Colossians 3:10-15

# TWENTY-SEVEN

# Getting Some Rest

*We, however, who have faith, shall reach a place of rest.*
Hebrews 4:3 (JB)

The letter to the Hebrews was written to encourage those who read it. Since they were God's chosen people, the author reminded them of their past, of a time when God was displeased with their ancestors because of their lack of faith. They were afraid to act when he called them into the promised land, so instead of entering, they wandered around in a desert for 40 years.

The author tells his friends that it was a failure of faith that caused this; and he says, *don't* imitate them. Believe, and you will enter into God's rest.

God's rest? What is that?

Most of us are far more interested in action. The idea of rest seems passive, maybe even uninteresting. Yet the idea of God's rest was not a passive thing at all, but rather a time of fulfillment, and it was directly tied up with faith. "Those who first heard the Good News did not go in and rest with God because they did not believe. There are, then, others who are allowed to receive it. This is shown by the fact that God sets another day, which is called 'Today' " (Heb 4:6-7).

What a strong image! The time for believing is *now*, this moment, "today." And by believing something happens, we enter into God's rest.

Rest from what?

103

According to Hebrews, whoever believes will rest from his own works, rest from the need to create oneself, one's existence (so that others will know who we are). Rest from the compulsive self which is constantly worried about whether it is liked, praised enough, admired, hated, or feared. Rest from the anger and greed which eats away at our energy and makes life miserable. Rest from what others think of us!

Perhaps it's true that there *are* only two emotions: one which we inherit and never leaves us, love; another, which the mind makes up, fear. From fear we judge, condemn, attack. Out of fear we compete with others for first place—and condemn ourselves when we lose. From fear comes the guilt that hounds us and won't let go. It has little to do with God and everything to do with self-justification! How good it would be to rest from all these negative emotions. How good to rest from the need to create and justify ourselves.

It is through faith that we rest from these things, for faith is a source of life. It *is* life-giving. Faith is a word of life spoken from the true self to God; and God, the source of life and love, speaks back, deep within the heart. That is what brings rest.

There is no rest in God, no fulfillment without faith. And faith comes from the heart. It's to the heart that God speaks, giving it rest.

"The word of God is alive and active, sharper than any double-edged sword. It cuts all the way through (the false self) to where soul and spirit meet, to where joints and marrow come together. It judges the desires and thoughts of a man's heart."

And the Lord said: Come to me all you who are burdened, and I shall give you rest. Take my burden on your shoulders. It is easy and light by comparison. And you shall find rest.

To come to God—*that* is the source of life. To rest in him is to be delivered from the false self. And this is a matter of the heart, of letting go of fear and the frantic energy we spend building up our own egos.

Psalm 95 vividly recalls the failure of heart the people of Israel had when they relied upon themselves and their own fears, disbelieving in God. They were going to run their lives the way *they* wanted, not the way God was inviting them to, which would have meant rest and fulfillment for them.

> Come, let us praise God
>    with joy,
>    for he is a rock,
>    our safety.
> Let us enter into his presence
>    filled with thanks,
>    for he is great
>    and rules gently over all that is!

He shaped the depths of the earth,
   the mountain tops,
   the sea—and all that lives.
*This* is our God!
And we? We are the people he pastures,
   like a shepherd looking out for his
   sheep.
He guides us with his hand.
If only you would listen to him today.
Don't harden your heart by worry and
   fear,
   as some have done,
   and then walked in the wilderness.
How unreliable they were.
They refused me,
   refused to discern my way with them.
So they failed to reach the place of rest
Which I prepared for them.

                    Psalm 95 (paraphrased)

# TWENTY-EIGHT

# Final Rest

*For if the dead are not raised, neither has Christ been raised.*
1 Corinthians 15:16

The man was grieving his younger brother's death. It had seemed so senseless: a life of promise not yet fulfilled cut off by cancer. He would rather it had been *his* life instead of his brother's. He had, after all, lived long enough to marry and raise a family. He knew his capabilities, had tested his talents—but his brother? He never made it past the age of 24.

The older man went into a deep depression and started to miss sleep. One night, long after the others had gone to bed, he wandered downstairs and into the kitchen. He opened the refrigerator door and after looking at the shelves decided nothing appealed to him. Turning toward the kitchen table, feeling dull and depressed, he said, "Maybe a cup of coffee would help." He eyed the stove. As he did, he felt a presence within the room. He looked upward as though he could find the reason for the presence there. At that moment he had a strong sense that his brother was in the room. Even stronger was the conviction that his brother was speaking to him. "It's all right, Frank. Everything is right, complete."

What was it? Who knows! But from that moment the depression ended. A great weight was lifted from his spirit, like that of a stone rolled back from the doorway of death, letting the sun stream in.

# TWENTY-NINE

# A Letter From Prison

*God is my witness that I tell you the truth when I say that my deep feeling for you all comes from the heart of Christ Jesus himself.*

Philippians 1:8

Paul wrote many letters to the early Christian churches. One, more than the others, stands out because it is so personal, so filled with joy, and it represents his mature understanding of the mystery and work of Jesus Christ. Paul wrote it to his friends, the people who lived in Philippi. The letter is also known as the epistle of joy because the word and the thought of joy are mentioned so many times.

The startling thing about this letter is that Paul wrote it while in prison—hardly the place one would expect to feel joy! Yet there must have been plenty of time to reflect; and maybe that's why the theme of joy surfaces so often: He was glad for his life and for his friends. Solitude can make us aware of such things. Solitude and prayer.

Listen to a few of the opening lines of this brief letter. He speaks of his friendship, a gift whose source is the heart of Christ.

I thank my God for you all every time I
think of you; and every time I pray for
you, I pray with joy. . . .
I am sure of this: that God, who began
this good work in you, will carry it on until it is finished in the day of Christ Jesus.

You are always in my heart! . . . So it
is right for me to feel this way about
you. . . . God knows that I tell the
truth when I say that my deep feeling
for you
comes from the heart of Christ Jesus
himself.

How much this says about the source of all deep
relationships! The heart of Christ brings them about
and carries them to perfection.

Of course! That is what you would expect, isn't it, if
God is love.

*Love is eternal.*

1 Corinthians 13:8

Both Sts. Augustine and Bernard taught that the
love that could end was never really love. The same, of
course, applies to friendship. The friendship that *could*
end was never really friendship.

The nature of love, it would seem, is *to be*, forever.
Certainly our songs reveal this, for we sing of love undying, never-ending, forever.

Way back in the instinctive zones of the spirit, we
recognize that love *should be* forever. And it's because of
that knowledge that we even talk about life everlasting.

It is inconceivable that God could once love us, then suddenly cease! Perhaps *we* might fail in this way, but not God.

Our hope for everlasting life is founded on the nature of love itself. That's why Paul wrote:

> For this reason I fall on my knees before the Father, from whom every family in heaven and on earth receives its true name. I ask God . . . to give you power through his Spirit to be strong in your inner selves, and I pray that Christ will make his home in your hearts through faith. I pray that you may have your roots and foundation in love, so that you, together with all God's people, may have the power to understand how broad and long, how high and deep, is Christ's love. Yes, may you come to know his love—although it can never be fully known—and so be completely filled with the very nature of God.
>
> Ephesians 3:14-19

# THIRTY

# The Love That Could End

What is God's love for us like? St. Paul speaks from the understanding and experience he had and taught at the very beginning of Christianity:

> Love is patient (God's love!) and kind; it is not jealous or conceited or proud; love is not ill-mannered or selfish or irritable; love does not keep a record of wrongs; love is not happy with evil, but is happy with the truth. Love never gives up, and its faith, hope, and patience never fail. Love is eternal.
>
> 1 Corinthians 13:4-8

It is as if the English language was invented in order to write this section of scripture. That is how beautiful it is. And what has such beauty must certainly touch upon a vein of truth.

If we wish to know how to think of God, how to picture him to our doubting minds, there is no better passage to start with than this one.

Try taking out the word "love" from the above quotation, and, in its place, put the name "Jesus Christ." You might then have an insight into the heart of Christ and his love for you.

111